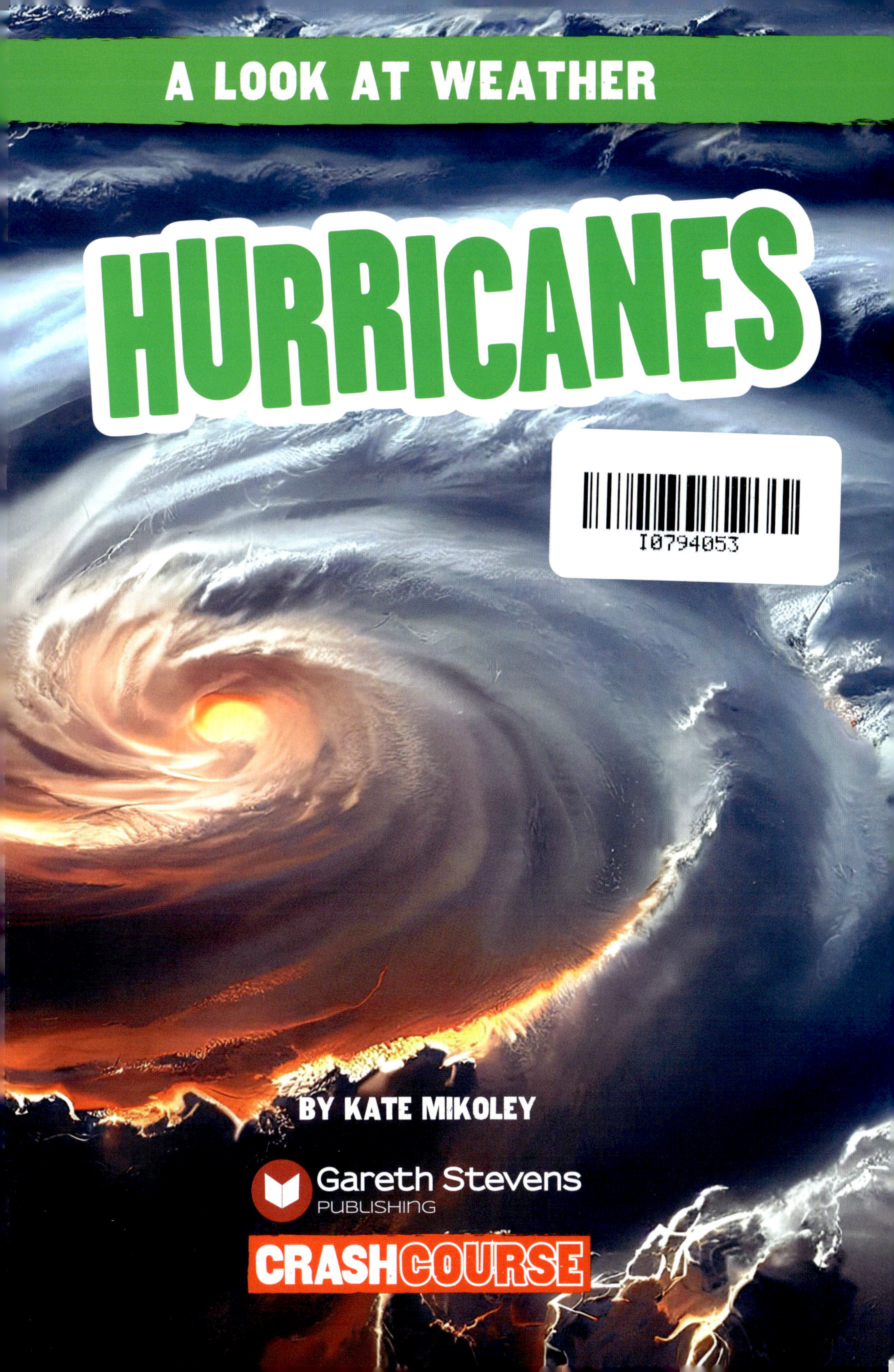

A LOOK AT WEATHER

HURRICANES

BY KATE MIKOLEY

Gareth Stevens PUBLISHING

CRASHCOURSE

Please visit our website, www.garethstevens.com. For a free color catalog of all our high-quality books, call toll free 1-800-542-2595 or fax 1-877-542-2596.

Cataloging-in-Publication Data

Names: Mikoley, Kate.
Title: Hurricanes / Kate Mikoley.
Description: New York : Gareth Stevens Publishing, 2024. | Series: A look at weather| Includes glossary, index, and bibliographic information
Identifiers: ISBN 9781538287286 (pbk) | ISBN 9781538287293 (library bound) | ISBN 9781538287309 (ebook)
Subjects: LCSH: Hurricanes-- Juvenile literature
Classification: LCC QC944.2 M55 2024 | DDC 551. 55/2--dc24

First Edition

Published in 2024 by
Gareth Stevens Publishing
2544 Clinton Street
Buffalo, NY 14224

Designer: Karen Quigley
Editor: Kate Mikoley

Photo credits: Cover, p. 1 Benny Marty/Shutterstock.com; warm/cold front symbols NickJulia/Shutterstock.com; cloud series art (cloud background) ekapol sirachainan/Shutterstock.com; series art (cartoon cloud) MimaCZ/Shutterstock.com; pp. 2-3 kzww/Shutterstock.com; p. 5 File:2022 Atlantic hurricane season summary map.png/Wikimedia Commons; p. 7 Mike Mareen/Shutterstock.com; p. 9 Terry Kelly/Shutterstock.com; p. 11 File:Tropical Depression 90C April 9, 2012.jpg/Wikimedia Commons; p. 13 Evgeniyqw/Shutterstock.com; p. 15 William A. Morgan/Shutterstock.com; p. 17 File:Tasman Sea (27990747076).jpg/Wikimedia Commons; p. 19 19 STUDIO/Shutterstock.com; p. 21 Trong Nguyen/Shutterstock.com; p. 23 File:Katrina-new-orleans-flooding3-2005.jpg/Wikimedia Commons; p. 25 imagedepotpro/iStock.com; p. 27 FashionStock.com/Shutterstock.com; p. 29 File:Hurricane Lane warning (29254459177).jpg/Wikimedia Commons.

Printed in the United States of America

CPSIA compliance information: Batch #CS24GS: For further information contact Gareth Stevens at 1-800-542-2595.

CONTENTS

Words in the glossary appear in **bold** type the first time they are used in the text.

A STORM AT SEA

The beach can be a restful and fun place. But it is not somewhere you want to be when a hurricane comes! Heavy winds and huge waves are signs this type of storm may be on its way.

Make the Grade

The Atlantic **basin**, which includes the Atlantic Ocean, Caribbean Sea, and Gulf of Mexico, gets about three **major** hurricanes a year.

tracking hurricanes in the Atlantic Ocean, 2022

Hurricanes are rotating, or spinning, storms that form over warm oceans. Hurricanes go by different names based on where they happen. Near Australia and the Indian Ocean, they're called cyclones. Near the Philippines, Japan, and China, they're called typhoons.

Make the Grade

These storms are called hurricanes when they happen around North America and the Caribbean.

No matter what you call them, hurricanes can be very dangerous. They can destroy, or ruin, buildings, such as people's homes. The strong winds can rip large trees out of the ground and knock down power lines. Huge waves and heavy rain can cause flooding.

Make the Grade

Some hurricanes happen at sea and cause no problems for people. Once they hit land, they can hurt whole communities.

FORMING A HURRICANE

All hurricanes start when rain and thunderstorms circle around in the ocean with low air **pressure**. This type of storm is called a **tropical** depression. If this happens in warm water, the tropical depression may get stronger and turn into a tropical storm or hurricane.

Make the Grade

Sea water needs to be at least 79°F (26°C) for a hurricane to form.

The low air pressure in a tropical depression causes the ocean air to rise up. This hot and **humid** air forms a **spiral** shape. Big clouds form. As more air gets sucked up, the spiral gets faster and stronger.

Make the Grade

A tropical depression becomes a tropical storm when wind speeds reach 39 miles (63 km) per hour. At 74 miles (119 km) per hour, it's a hurricane.

FUELING THE STORM

Warm water is like **fuel** for a hurricane. If the storm moves over cool water, it may stop before reaching land. When a hurricane does hit land, it will lose some power without warm water to fuel it. Still, hurricanes can cause a lot of problems before stopping.

Make the Grade

A storm surge is when huge waves of ocean water are pushed to the shore. These can be more than 20 feet (6 m) high and reach many miles **inland**.

WHEN AND WHERE?

Hurricanes commonly happen in the summer or fall. In the Northern **Hemisphere**, which is where the United States is, hurricane season is between June and November. In the Southern Hemisphere, they happen between December and April.

Make the Grade

Seasons happen at different times in the Northern and Southern Hemispheres because of Earth's **tilt**. This is why the two halves of the planet have different hurricane seasons.

THE EYE OF THE STORM

You may hear people talk about the "eye" of a hurricane. This is the center of the stormy spiral. It is still and quiet here. Air pressure is low, and there are clear skies. But it is in the middle of the storm!

Make the Grade

Inside the hurricane's eye, it might seem like the storm is over. But as the storm moves, the other side of the spiral brings back heavy winds and rain.

WHAT'S IN A NAME?

In the United States, tropical storms are given names. The first storm of the season gets a name that starts with the letter A. The following storms get names that start with the next letters of the alphabet until the end of the season.

Make the Grade

The U.S. National Weather Service has a list of names it goes through every six years. However, names of really bad storms are retired, or removed, from the list.

ONE TERRIBLE STORM

Hurricane Katrina hit the U.S. coast of the Gulf of Mexico in 2005. It caused bad flooding in Louisiana, destroyed buildings, and killed more than 1,800 people. It was the deadliest U.S. hurricane since 1928.

Make the Grade

As of 2022, Hurricane Katrina is the costliest **natural disaster** in U.S. history.

STORM CATEGORIES

Hurricanes are rated on a scale of 1 to 5. Each of these ratings is called a category. A Category 1 hurricane has wind speeds of 74 to 95 miles (119 to 153 km) per hour. A Category 5 reaches speeds of 157 miles (252 km) per hour or more.

Make the Grade

The scale used to rate hurricanes is called the Saffir-Simpson Hurricane Wind Scale. Category 3 storms and higher are considered major hurricanes.

Hurricanes can result in deaths no matter their category. Other things, such as rainfall and **storm surges**, add to how unsafe a hurricane is. Even tropical storms and depressions can ruin buildings and hurt people.

Make the Grade

Any category of hurricane can result in power loss.

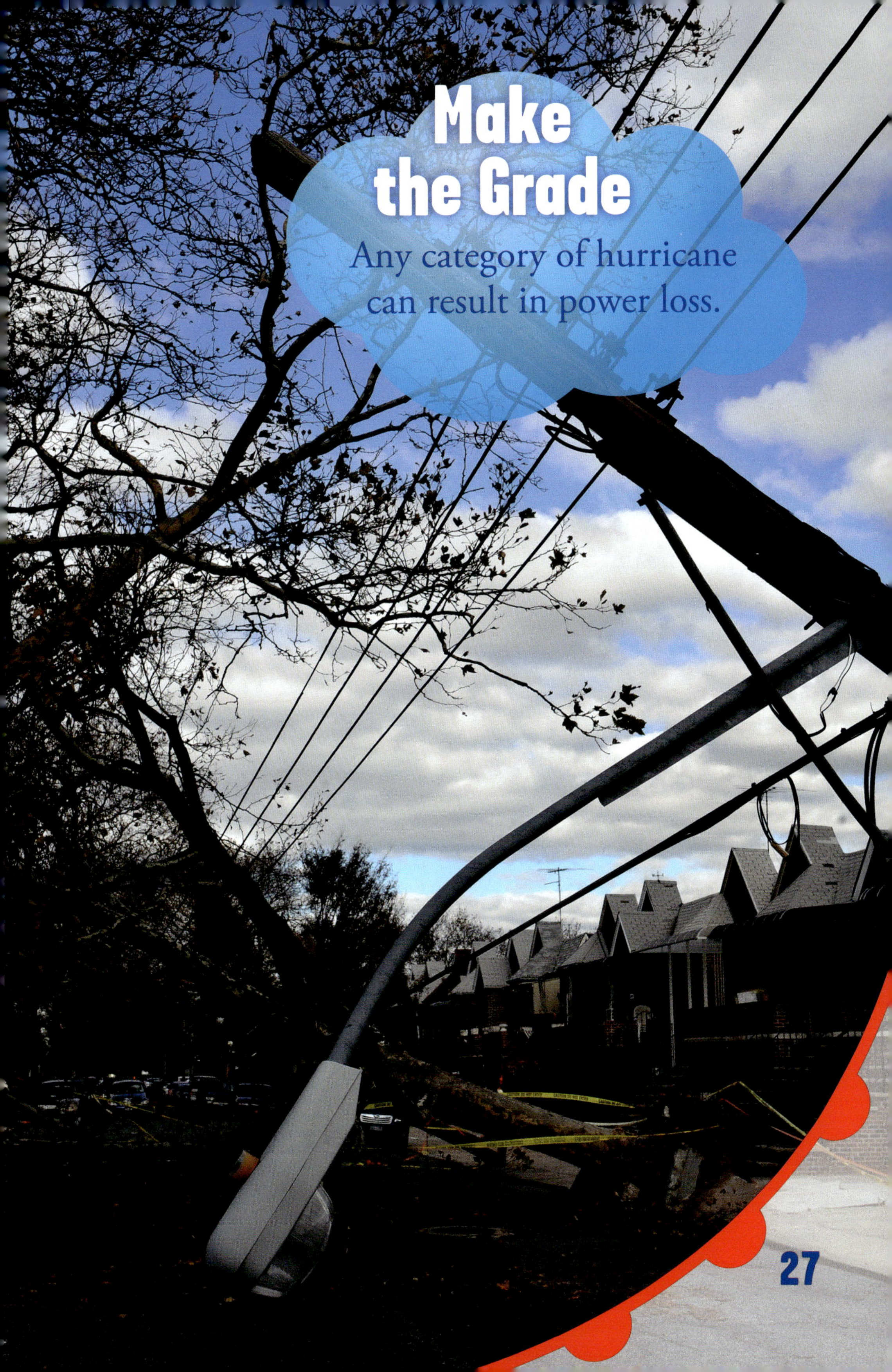

STAYING SAFE

If a hurricane is headed your way, it is important to listen to scientists and government officials. They may suggest you board up windows and leave your town. Large buildings, such as schools, are often used as safe places for those in need of somewhere to stay.

Make the Grade

Scientists can tell if a hurricane is coming. If one is headed your way and there's time to do so safely, it's often best to go to a place the storm won't reach.

THE SAFFIR-SIMPSON HURRICANE WIND SCALE

Category	Wind Speed
1	74-95 miles (119-153 km) per hour
2	96-110 miles (154-177 km) per hour
3	111-129 miles (178-208 km) per hour
4	130-156 miles (209-251 km) per hour
5	157 miles (252 km) or faster

GLOSSARY

basin: A dip in the Earth's surface, somewhat shaped like a bowl.

fuel: Something used to make energy, heat, or power.

hemisphere: One-half of Earth.

humid: Containing moisture.

inland: The inner part of a country.

major: Great or important.

natural disaster: A sudden, terrible event in nature that results in serious harm and many deaths.

pressure: A force that pushes on something else.

spiral: A shape or line that curls outward from a center point.

storm surge: The rising of ocean water because of a storm.

tilt: A position that is not straight up and down.

tropical: Having to do with the warm parts of Earth near the equator.

FOR MORE INFORMATION

BOOKS

Lew, Kristi. *Hurricanes*. New York, NY: Britannica Educational Publishing, 2019.

London, Martha. *Hurricanes*. Minneapolis, MN: DiscoverRoo, 2020.

WEBSITE

Hurricanes
kids.nationalgeographic.com/science/article/hurricane
This article has lots of facts about hurricanes, as well as tips on how to stay safe during one.

Publisher's note to educators and parents: Our editors have carefully reviewed these websites to ensure that they are suitable for students. Many websites change frequently, however, and we cannot guarantee that a site's future contents will continue to meet our high standards of quality and educational value. Be advised that students should be closely supervised whenever they access the internet.

INDEX